A Second Helping of Del'ISHcious 'ISH!

REGINA GRIFFIN

EDITED BY M. FRANCES SCOTT
PHOTOGRAPHY BY TONY SMART

'ISHues Vol II
A Second Helping of Del'ISHcious 'Ish!

ISBN 13: 978-1-4700370-5-5
LCCN: 2012902910
First Edition
1 2 3 4 5 6 7 8 9 10

Humor / General

For information, please contact:

GRIFFIN SCOTT
PRESS

www.GriffinScott.Press.com

★

In His divinity, God will sometimes especially appoint an
angel to your watch.
An angel who soothes every burden . . .
shields every pain . . .
comforts every ache . . .
accompanies every journey . . .
anticipates every need . . .
An angel who catches you when you're falling from the
weight of life's woes.

Marc Anthony, you are mine.

I cannot thank you enough.
I love you Que-boo!

★

Acknowledgements

★

After writing my first book "Ish" (VOL I), it didn't take long to realized the sales stream evaporates pretty quickly after all your friends and family purchase five copies. My brain taunted, "What now?" Before I could confront the daunting question with a game plan, my circle of life responded with an underground swell of support. Friends began to tell other friends, family members and coworkers about "Ish" and my book signings. They helped spread the word through Facebook, Twitter and so many other outlets— getting the book as far and wide as word of mouth could travel. This unbreakable, unrelenting, loyalty and staunch support has made "Ishues" (VOL II) possible. I am grateful, humbled and revitalized to see what this new journey will bring, and have so many of you to thank.

I praise and honor my Lord and Savior for paving the way and lighting my path. He continuously fortifies me during the times I have felt like stopping or retreating. He keeps pushing me out front as living example that "all things are possible" with HIM! Thank you Jesus!

I thank my mommy who is my rock, amour, cheerleader, confidant, advocate, gentle critic and oh yeah . . . editor! I love you mommy! I would NEVER want to do this without you.

My sister and brother (Vivian and Keith Griffin) support me in ways that tire me from just watching. Vivian birthed my cover muse Carrie Frances, who swears she's coauthor of the books. HA! My baby brother, Adrian Keith, flew a whole day from the Middle East to surprise me at a book signing. There is no bond like that of biological siblings. I need you sissy and baby brother to stay connected to the ways of our rearing. Stay close to me always.

My best friend Teresa Wietzikoski, personally put my book in the hands of her enormous client base and shamelessly plugged "Ish" to anyone willing to listen. She and her husband Richard, hosted my first book release party in their home, adorned with overwhelming love and beauty. My deepest gratitude to both of you!

My resident divas, Phyllis Bryant and Latoya Crenshaw hold me down every, single book signing in my hometown. You give up your Saturdays to support and grace my signing table with their fabulousness (coordinating your wardrobe to match the color theme—EVERYTIME). You both have blessed me in ways that are unspeakable. We share a bond that nothing can penetrate.

Tony Smart, my fantastically talented and patient photographer, you allow my niece and me to wreak havoc on your studio for our cover shoots. You are a saint and never fail at making us look our absolute best.

Ted Ruybal of Bluetail Books, your beautiful mind brought to life my revision of "Ish" Volume I and the new vision for "Ishues." You are extraordinary and the "Rain man" of illustration.

My Albany family and loved ones, you stopped the daily grind of your lives and traveled with passion to support my dream. You are a force and together we are a solid unit of oneness—FAMILY!

My SILS, Sabrena Alvin and Jameca Barrett, you love me in spite of my shortcomings and only manage to see the big in me. Please know I treasure the connection we share. Our love for one another slays any drama.

My Lakeshore Lancer and Morris Brown Wolverine family, your support and turnout is always a tear-jerking moment. Lancers are always "loyal and true." Wolverines, "hail to thee dear Morris Brown."

To my fabulously insane circle of friends

Justina Houston, you are my sister, roadie and Ted's companion for life! KKM is the coolest circle of women on earth!

Pamela Johnson, you deserve an hourly fee for the hours of talking me out of "dark and scary places." WHEW!

Rosalyn Williams, you are the heartbeat of my sanity and

the prom queen I always wanted to be. Stay wrapped in HIS word, sweetheart.

Vickie Mitchell, you somehow found the bedazzled, pink "Ish lips" ring that I wear in all my media pictures. Love it, love it, love it! Love you!

Sherry "Sham" Leetham, you were my first Amazon sale! I bow down to you!

Terri Ewing purchased 15 books and was my first book club signing. Thank you for believing in me enough to dish the 'Ish with your club.

Billy Briggs, you put the 'Ish on the air waves and I ain't mad atcha! Firm Radio reigns!

Tosha Love Vinson provided my beautiful jewelry for the "Ishues" book release party. You are a goddess.

Wendy Rae Miller and Aida Techilo (my stylists), you keep my tresses "bossy" and camera ready. YEAH BABY!

Peter "RHOA" Thomas hosted the "Ishues" release party at his swank, Atlanta BarOne. Your graciousness and hospitality will not be forgotten.

I extend my greatest, biggest, widest, deepest appreciation to each of you and especially the unnamed. You are all poignant chapters in the book of my journey. This is only the beginning.

Keep Dishin' the 'Ishues,

Regina

★

'ISH - (n.) ish

1. A random, eclectic statement intended to provoke emotion—whether laughter, frustration, happiness or angst

2. Statement creating a gust of thought

3. A wanton expression or point of view

'ISHues - (n.) ish-oos

1. Subjects of significant concern

2. Matters of arguable debate

3. Hot topics

'Ish #161

★

Put some 'Ish (Volume I)
in your life!

'Ish #162

★

Must you talk so loudly on your cell phone? I don't care that your bowels didn't move this morning.

'Ish #163

★

It wasn't a cruise if you started
in Ft. Lauderdale and ended
in Miami.

'Ish #164

★

Lie – (v.) a desperate action taken when repercussion of the truth is feared.

'Ish #165

★

Spinning pinky rings are for pimps, *not pastors.*

'Ish #166

★

Unless you're Lou Rawls, concede
that hamburger meat on your chest
is not sexy.

'Ish #167

★

The first and last of everything
is special.
Cherish it.
Especially children!

'Ish #168

★

Never endorse a politician who
carries one-hundred singles
at any given time.

'Ish #169

★

If one person has done it,
it's not impossible.
If no one has done it,
make it possible.

'Ish #170

★

Stop giving advice
you would never use.

'Ish #171

★

Ignorance is defined as looking for oyster crackers *on an oyster bar.*

'Ish #172

★

Luck is where purpose
meets destiny.

'Ish #173

★

The gift of giving is rooted
in abandoning all expectations
to receive.

'Ish #174

★

LIVE NOW!
Every life has an expiration date.

'Ish #175

★

Use jealousy as fuel and
motivation to create success
in your own life.

'Ish #176

★

Parting your lips softly during a job interview is not enough to camouflage your sterling silver tongue ring.

'Ish #177

★

You never know what you don't know, *until you finally know it.*

'Ish #178

★

Your life's meaning is told in the SUM of your life's decisions, *not just the bad ones.*

'Ish #179

★

Rule makers are mostly followers.
Rule breakers are most
always geniuses.

'Ish #180

★

You say you have faith,
but why can't anyone tell?
Believing is seeing.

'Ish #181

★

Therapy is not shameful . . .
needing and refusing it is.

'Ish #182

★

Fly swatters are so 1965.
Close the windows and
turn on the AC.

'Ish #183

★

A barely furnished apartment is not a swank bachelor's pad. It's really just a **barely furnished** apartment. Nice try.

'Ish #184

★

Prepare a romantic fondue dinner
for your sweetie and eat it in
the middle of the living room
on a picnic table cloth.

'Ish #185

★

Put more effort into *being* than *pretending* to be.

'Ish #186

★

If your personal trainer wears
a super reinforced girdle
(aka . . . MAN SPANX) . . .
you need a new trainer.

'Ish #187

★

Awareness and admission are the first steps toward recovery.

'Ish #188

★

If Nelson Mandela rose above being innocently imprisoned for 27 years, *what the hell are you complaining about?*

'Ish #189

★

Dating someone who is already
married isn't infidelity,
it's inhumane.

'Ish #190

★

Eight inch heels aren't stilettos,
they're stripper stilts.

'Ish #191

★

RECIPE FOR A SUCCESSFUL
RELATIONSHIP:
One pulls.
The other stretches.
BOTH GROW!

'Ish #192

★

Any deal described as a
"ground floor, once in a lifetime
opportunity . . ."
ISN'T!

'Ish #193

★

A legitimate parking valet attendant
will never ask if your
"house key is the round one."

'Ish #194

★

Cocaine is not an elitist's drug
of choice.
It's an idiot's drug of choice!

'Ish #195

★

Ask, "How are you?" to a stranger . . .
and really mean it.

'Ish #196

★

Give to your child what was
taken from you.

'Ish #197

★

If you can't change your abusive
spouse, **change your spouse!**

'Ish #198

★

It's a buffet, *not a bonanza.*
You've been at the table for 8 hours.
Please go home!

'Ish #199

★

He who possesses self-control
and restraint is the victor
in any argument.

'Ish #200

★

Stop **wishing!**
Start **expecting!**

'Ish #201

★

Take your grandparents to dinner
in the middle of the week.

'Ish #202

★

If something told you not to do it . . .
WHY'D YOU DO IT?

'Ish #203

★

There's good in everyone . . .
some just have it buried down a tad
further than others.

'Ish #204

★

Stop saying it's baby weight
if your baby is in his third year
of college.

'Ish #205

★

Granite counter tops and hardwood floors **are not** smart investments for a double-wide trailer.

'Ish #206

★

A solid relationship is like a good
bowl of sweet and sour soup.
The bitter elements make the sweet
even *better.*

'Ish #207

★

He who enforces the rules must also
follow the rules.
Practice what you impose.

'Ish #208

★

Live a life that makes the world miss
you when you're gone.

'Ish #209

★

Myth: Six black German Shepherds
smoking cigars, playing pool
in dashikis (matted on maroon,
crushed, velvet canvas) is *not*
Black art.

'Ish #210

★

Stay out of drive through windows.
Go home and cook!
Your thighs and wallet
will thank you.

'Ish #211

★

Your child is your parental obligation, *not friend.*

'Ish #212

★

Stop using straw from the broom
stick to pick food out of your teeth.
THAT'S SUPER DISGUSTING!

'Ish #213

★

It's delusional to judge wealth
by your income.
Wealth is ultimately determined
by your rate of consumption versus
accumulation.

'Ish #214

★

He's not your boyfriend if you don't
know where he lives.
Just saying.

'Ish #215

★

Listening to your iPod while
standing in front of the television
for 30 minutes is not exercising.

'Ish #216

★

You live in an $800,000 house.
You don't need a screen on the
front door!

'Ish #217

★

If it's all about gifts, *it's not Christmas you're celebrating.*

'Ish #218

★

Wisdom is doing,
not knowing.

'Ish #219

★

Take a vacation every year,
even if it's a stay-cation.

'Ish #220

★

Spend 15 minutes on crazy, then get back to normal. People won't even notice you had a nervous breakdown.

'Ish #221

★

Stop writing checks the day
BEFORE your pay day!

'Ish #222

★

Don't discount the advice of people who have not **birthed** children. Wisdom and life experiences are given to all.

'Ish #223

★

Even though you have 45 hours
of home study and an online
certificate of completion
in neurological science . . .
you will **STILL** *need a license
to practice medicine.*

'Ish #224

★

Good friendships can be an
occasional inconvenience, but good
friends honor the occasion.

'Ish #225

★

A couple's bubble bath is
for soaking not bathing,
unless you like bathing in dirt.

'Ish #226

★

Our children grow up to be
reflections of our abundance . . .
and deficits.

'Ish #227

★

No matter what people
in the world tell you . . .
you are enough!

'Ish #228

★

NO! Banana leaves don't taste anything like bananas.

'Ish #229

★

You can't sail the seven seas . . .
if you don't leave the safety
of the shores.
LIVE!

'Ish #230

★

Use fewer words to make a point
more effectively.

'Ish #231

★

YES!
Phone and internet sex
IS infidelity . . .
when you're married.

'Ish #232

★

Using *69 to call back hang-ups
is asinine.
If they wanted to talk they wouldn't
have hung up!

'Ish #233

★

If you find yourself in a sexless
relationship, your partner
is probably sexing someone else.

'Ish #234

★

Your posture says a lot about
your self-esteem.
Sit up straight!

'Ish #235

★

Do a 7-day cleanse the first week
in January . . . *every year.*

'Ish #236

★

When you encounter a restaurant
that has menus with no pricing . . .
run like hell.

'Ish #237

★

Take a transatlantic cruise!
It's the easiest way to visit 8 cities
in 3 countries in 12 days.

'Ish #238

★

End all things good . . . *especially relationships.*

'Ish #239

★

Excessive flatulence is the mother of all underwear turtle tracks.

'Ish #240

★

Ok, ok, ok!!!
You ran your high school varsity
team's winning touchdown for
87 yards
... *in 1964.*
It's 2012!
GET A LIFE.

'Ish #241

★

At the end of each day, fill
a piggy bank with all your
pocket change.
Use the money for your next
vacation.

'Ish #242

★

Give your lover a pet name **you** can only use in *complete* privacy.

'Ish #243

★

Leave the world your very best.
Die empty.

'Ish #244

★

If your new girlfriend is the same age as your youngest daughter, you're not a player. **YOU'RE A PERVERT.**

'Ish #245

★

I know you paid $5,000 for your computer, but it's 10 years old. Stop paying for repairs and get a friggin' new one!

'Ish #246

★

Family members can be easy to love,
but hard to like.

'Ish #247

★

Get off your damn cell phone
at the dinner table!

'Ish #248

★

"Second place" is really just a polite title for 1st place dud.

'Ish #249

★

Who's your daddy?
No really!
Who is your daddy?

'Ish #250

★

It's probably not a good idea to use
your neighbor's hysterectomy pain
killers for your toothache.

'Ish #251

★

Stop making new friendships
when you aren't servicing your
existing ones.

'Ish #252

★

Every life has SIGNIFICANT
meaning.
FIND YOURS!

'Ish #253

★

IOU's don't have
expiration dates.

'Ish #254

★

Chronicle your child's life
with photographs.

'Ish #255

★

Dental floss is for gums and teeth . . .
not beach and poolside.

'Ish #256

★

If your warm-up suit stayed on 90%
of the season, stop telling people you
PLAY professional ball.

'Ish #257

★

Never leave a job without extending two weeks' notice, regardless of circumstance. *Please disregard if you hit the Powerball!*

'Ish #258

★

The less information you know
about people, the less drama you
have to manage.
Stay oblivious!

'Ish #259

★

The world is bigger than your
front door.
Explore other countries, cultures,
races and religions.

'Ish #260

★

Stop bragging that you haven't had a physical in ten years. The consolation prize for your stupidity is a marble, engraved headstone.

'Ish #261

★

Learn to speak the unwritten language of the generations before and after yours.

'Ish #262

★

SUBMISSION to God is
PROTECTION from God.

'Ish #263

★

LIKING (not loving) your spouse is the key to great love making.

'Ish #264

★

Positioning a telescope into your
neighbor's bedroom is probably
against the law.

'Ish #265

★

If you can't pronounce it,
don't order it.
In fact, why are you even in
that restaurant?

'Ish #266

★

No distance can separate true love,
if it does,
maybe it isn't love.

'Ish #267

★

A woman can NEVER
smell too good.

'Ish #268

★

Your gut instinct is God's whisper
to you.
TRUST IT.

'Ish #269

★

The unhealed emotional **cracks** in your life will create emotional **canyons** in your children.

'Ish #270

★

Start exercising three times a week
this year and run a half marathon
next year.

'Ish #271

★

A hard heart leads to an easy divorce.

'Ish #272

★

Change is temporary.
Transformation is permanent.
Ask a butterfly.

'Ish #273

★

If the airlines wanted you to have
a meal, they would have included
it in your fare.
**No, you can't have extra cookies
and peanuts!**

'Ish #274

★

Fathering a child makes you
a sperm donor.
Loving and rearing a child makes
you a dad.

'Ish #275

★

The past is gone forever.
The power lies in the present.

'Ish #276

★

Drive to the mountains,
see the changing of the leaves,
stay the weekend in a cabin,
leave your laptop at home,
and turn off your cell phone.

'Ish #277

★

Women create the world.
Really!
How many men do you know
with uteruses?
Wait . . . don't answer that!

'Ish #278

★

When you go through life in denial,
you can NEVER fully be the person
God intended.

'Ish #279

★

Your birthday is one day,
but the celebration should last
one week.

'Ish #280

★

Stop wishing you were younger and start using the hard earned lessons to build a purposed and wiser existence.

'Ish #281

★

If your child is in the tenth grade
and reads on a third grade level,
it's your fault,
not the school system's.

'Ish #282

★

Don't make a decision if you can't
bear the consequences it brings.

'Ish #283

★

Sometimes what you love
about a person is also what
you hate.

'Ish #284

★

Hire a maid service to do your spring cleaning and spend the weekend at a cozy bed and breakfast.

'Ish #285

★

If your therapist is a chain smoker
and has involuntary face twitches,
switch seats.

'Ish #286

★

If he takes an hour longer to get
dressed and his favorite color
is fuchsia, your June wedding
is probably not a good idea.

'Ish #287

★

You don't win by DEBATING
who you are.
You win by LIVING who you are.

'Ish #288

★

Every member of your family was
hand-picked by God.
Love and honor **HIS** selections.

'Ish #289

★

If it's not the whole truth,
it's a lie.

'Ish #290

★

Wish. Believe. Pray. Wait.
RECEIVE!

'Ish #291

★

There is no exhaustion like that of having a codependent lover.

'Ish #292

★

Geniuses are born, not created in classrooms.

'Ish #293

★

Unaddressed dysfunctionalism
eventually begins to feel normal . . .
which is abnormal.

'Ish #294

★

Apologize!
You stubborn bull.

'Ish #295

★

A low-fat hot dog on a bun with hydrogenated fat, baked potato chips with MSG and a tall glass of unsweetened green iced tea with saccharine is NOT a healthy lunch.

'Ish #296

★

Fall in love,
get married
and start a family.
Note to self . . . . . .
the ordering is not random.

'Ish #297

★

Enjoy a slice of hot, flaky pie with
a bowl of homemade ice cream,
*and bring an extra spoon for
your honey.*

'Ish #298

★

Rebuke the language of **lack:**
CAN'T . . .
WON'T . . .
IF . . .

'Ish #299

★

Speak the language of
abundance:
CAN . . .
WILL . . .
WHEN . . .

'Ish #300

★

I don't think you can call the day
you met an ANNIVERSARY,
if you're his mistress.

'Ish #301

★

Stop pretending to be picky and asking "Who made the green bean casserole?" You made the meatloaf out of potted meat!

141

'Ish #302

★

If you show up to work around noon
and plan to leave before five, you
don't get a lunch break.
*You obviously took it before
arriving.*

'Ish #303

★

It's a street food vendor!
Stop asking for the health
score ratings.

'Ish #304

★

Ladies, your brother and father
can NEVER be present for
natural birthing.
That's not family bonding . . .
that's family creepy!

'Ish #305

★

If your mama said it,
believe it!

Introducing the 'Ish Master

★

Regina Griffin is the author of "Ish - Getting the 'Ish out in the Open," and its spicy follow up, "ISHues - A Second Helping of Del'ishcious Ish." Inspired by pithy, memorable phrases she saw stenciled on the wall of a department store and her own life's follies, Griffin crafted the collection of provoking sayings. The explosive culmination is two books of page-turning, gut-busting, make-you-wanna-say . . . uuuuum expressions

Regina Griffin is a native of Atlanta, Georgia who holds a bachelor's degree in Broadcast Journalism. Her former writing credentials include editor's choice blogger, contributing writer for *The Atlanta Journal & Constitution's Intown* newspaper and speech writer for a former Commissioner of Public Safety.

This entrepreneur has recently added the titles of author and publisher to her long list of professional credentials. A working author, Regina enjoys connecting with readers. She spends the majority of her time traveling the country, dishin' the 'Ish at book signings, speaking engagements and media venues.

'Ish - Vol I is available where books are sold
and online for all e-readers.

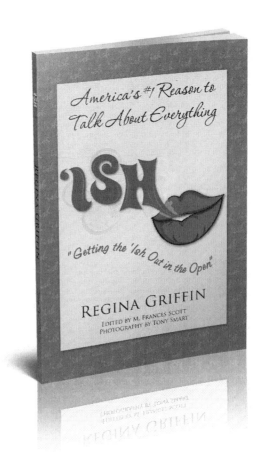

Griffin Scott Press

www.GriffinScott.Press.com

11659468R00092

Made in the USA
Charleston, SC
12 March 2012